The

Gospels

Compared and Contrasted

W M Henry & Michael Penny

ISBN: 978-1-78364-441-4

The Open Bible Trust
Fordland Mount, Upper Basildon,
Reading, RG8 8LU, UK.

www.obt.og.uk

Contents

Introduction 7

Section 1: The Gospel Writers and their aims 11

- The writers 13
- The aims of the gospel writers 18

Section 2: Comparing the Gospels 27

- The central themes 27
- The King and the Kingdom proclaimed 33
- The King and the Kingdom rejected 38
- The Climax of the Gospels 42
- The Lord's miracles 48
- The Lord's titles 50

Section 3: Contrasting the Gospels 57

- Contrasts in common incidents in the synoptic gospels 57
- Luke's emphasis on the outsider 63
- The unique approach of the fourth Gospel 68

Conclusion 75

Appendix: The Dating of the Gospels 81

More on the Gospels 85

About the authors 86

Also by W M Henry and Michael Penny 89

Further Reading: Galatians 90

About this book 91

Introduction

Introduction

In our Bibles we have four different records of the Lord's earthly ministry. No doubt many other records of this unique time in human history were written, as Luke explains to Theophilus in the opening verse of his gospel.

> Many have undertaken to draw up an account of the things that have been fulfilled among us, just as they were handed down to us by those who from the first were eyewitnesses and servants of the word. (Luke 1:1-2)

Some of the accounts were careful and meticulous, like that of Luke (see Luke 1:3-4) while others were sensationalist, apocryphal and inconsistent in their treatment of the Lord's actions and teaching. The compilers of the New Testament prayerfully reviewed the manuscripts available and concluded that the four gospels now in our possession present an accurate picture of the Lord and His work while He lived on the earth.

So what is the message that they bring to us? There are many similarities between them – particularly the first three gospels – and they all portray a consistent picture of the Lord and His work. However, there are also significant differences between them since the four writers were very different individuals. Matthew and John were two of the Lord's disciples and describe what they saw for themselves. Mark, who did encounter the Lord during His ministry, was not one of The Twelve, but, traditionally learned a great deal from Peter. Luke, a Gentile, came on the scene later and was a close companion of Paul.

The four writers also had different readerships in mind and therefore there are variations in emphasis. Some gospels describe incidents which are omitted from others. However, in other cases, there are different nuances in the way the same incidents are presented, as the writers try to identify particular lessons for their readers.

This publication tries both to compare and contrast the four gospel records. Who were the writers and what were their aims? What are the common themes of the gospels and how do they present a consistent portrait of Christ? What are the essential differences between the gospels and why are these differences present?

This look at the four Gospels is divided into three sections. The opening section discusses what we know about the gospel writers and their distinctive aims. The second section compares the four gospel records, setting out the common themes of the gospels and their similarities. In the final section we will explore the differences between the gospels and consider why these differences exist. In this way it is hoped to build up a rounded picture of the Lord's earthly ministry, the events in His life, and what He taught and did.

Section 1: The Gospel Writers and their aims

Section 1: The Gospel Writers and their aims

The usual way of comparing the four gospels is to first look at the three synoptic gospels (Matthew, Mark and Luke) as giving a unified view of Christ, His life and teaching, and then to compare those with John.

The first three gospels compared

There is a great deal of common content in the synoptic gospels. Mark is generally regarded as the source gospel and both Matthew and Luke use him extensively.

Graham Scroggie[1] observes that Matthew contains the substance of 606 out of Mark's 661 verses and the figure for Luke is 320. The small amount of material unique to Mark's Gospel includes three healing miracles and the parable of the seed growing secretly (Mark 4:26-29). In addition, Mark alone records the incident of the young man escaping naked from Gethsemane.

There is also a great deal of common material between Matthew and Luke, some of which has been taken from Mark, but there is other common material which appears to have come from an unknown document[2] which theologians call "Q". However, although the three gospels cover a great deal of common events and teaching, there is a considerable difference in emphasis in the way they do so and this will be addressed later in the booklet.

---

[1] W Graham Scroggie, *A Guide to the Gospels*, Pickering & Inglis, 1973, p132 & 248.
[2] Or document<u>s</u>; see Luke 1:1

The relationship between the first three and the fourth gospel

John's Gospel is very different from the other three. Westcott stated that 92% of the content of the fourth gospel is unique to it. Another commentator suggested that apart from the Passion narrative, the only incidents common to all four gospels are:

- Christ feeding the 5,000;
- Christ walking on water;
- Christ's anointing by Mary

If these two views are correct, then this section comparing the four gospels will be very brief. However, if we stand back from the detail in these writings and take a broader view of the four, we might have a different, and better, picture.

The writers

The writers of the four gospels were very different people.

Matthew

Matthew was one of the twelve disciples (see e.g. Matthew 10:3). He was also called Levi and was the son of Alphaeus (Mark 2:14). He was a Jew but worked as a tax collector for the Roman authorities. In fact, Matthew 9:9 and Mark 2:14-17 and Luke 5:27-28 describe the Lord Jesus calling Matthew to follow Him as he sat in his tax collector's booth. Matthew immediately rose up and followed and we read of a subsequent dinner at his house, which was attended by some of his colleagues. Jews who worked for the Romans were regarded as traitors and were despised by the people. Matthew, Mark and Luke's accounts of the feast at Matthew's house all record the complaints of the Pharisees that the Lord was eating with 'tax collectors and sinners.'

It is perhaps surprising that such an individual was prepared to become a follower of the Lord Jesus, who was perceived as Israel's Messiah. There is little doubt that the disciples, up until the resurrection, saw Jesus' Messianic role as being primarily political and anticipated that He would overthrow the Romans, and restore Israel's kingdom. One wonders how a 'traitor' like Matthew could work alongside 'Simon the Zealot,' who was also one of the twelve. 'James, son of Alphaeus' (Mark 3:18) was another disciple and it could be that he and Matthew were brothers, though there is nothing in the text to indicate this. Matthew's Gospel presents the Lord Jesus very much as the fulfiller of Israel's expectations and perhaps Matthew wanted to break away from the compromising position he was in. Matthew does, however, remain very much in the background and, although he is included in all the listings of the disciples in the gospels and Acts, there is no other mention of him in the Scriptures.

Mark

John Mark was also a Jew and lived in Jerusalem. His mother, Mary, appears to have been a woman of wealth who had become a Christian. Her house was used as a meeting place for the church (Acts 12:12) and when Peter was released from prison, that was where he went. There is no mention of Mark in the gospels, although it has been suggested that the he was young man in Mark 14:51-52, who followed Jesus into Gethsemane and only escaped the soldiers by leaving his linen garment in their hands. However, this is not certain.

What is known is that he was a cousin of Barnabas (Colossians 4:10) and accompanied Barnabas and Paul on their missionary journey recorded in Acts 13. When they reached Pamphylia, Mark left them (Acts 13:13) and did not continue in the work. Subsequently, when Barnabas wanted to take Mark with them on a second journey, Paul refused because he had let them down before and this caused Barnabas and Paul to split, with Barnabas taking Mark with him to Cyprus and Paul taking Silas and going to Syria and Cilicia (Acts 15:39-41). However, Mark does seem to have redeemed himself because Paul, writing to Timothy in what is probably his last letter, asks Timothy to:

> Get Mark and bring him with you, because he is helpful to me in my ministry (2 Timothy 4:11)

In 1 Peter 5:13, he is described as "my son Mark" and it has been suggested by second century Christian writers that he was "the interpreter of Peter" and that much of the material recorded in Mark's Gospel comes from Peter. However, this is not certain and Mark does appear to have worked closely with both Peter and Paul.

Luke

Luke was the writer of the third gospel and also the Acts of the Apostles. Both books are addressed to Theophilus and Acts 1:1-2 refers back to "my former book," which contained details of "all that Jesus began to do and to teach until the day he was taken up into heaven." Luke was a doctor and, although not one of the twelve disciples, travelled extensively with Paul. Many of the descriptions of Paul's journeys in Acts bear the stamp of an eye-witness and some sections (e.g. Acts chapters 16, 20 and 27) speak of Paul and his companions as 'we,' indicating Luke's presence with them.

It is apparent from Acts that Luke had a huge admiration for Paul and it appears that this feeling was mutual. Paul refers to Luke in Colossians 4:14 describing him as "our dear friend Luke the doctor." So Luke was with Paul in his first imprisonment in Rome. In his last letter Paul sadly observes that "only Luke is with me" (2 Timothy 4:11), so Luke's loyalty to the great apostle continued to the end. Luke appears to have been a Gentile since, in Colossians 4, Paul names Aristarchus, Mark and Jesus who is called Justus as "the only Jews among my fellow-workers for the kingdom of God" (verses 10-11). We know from verse 14 that Luke was also with Paul, so he must have been a Gentile.
There is nothing to indicate that Luke had been present during the Lord's ministry and he states at the start of his gospel that what he has written is the result of careful research so that his reader, Theophilus, might be assured of the accuracy of the things he had been taught (Luke 1:3-4).

John

John is the second-most prolific writer in the New Testament, producing three short epistles and the book of Revelation, in addition to his gospel. He was the son of Zebedee and brother of James. Zebedee ran a family fishing business which included "hired men" (Mark 1:20), so they were probably a wealthy family with ambitious aspirations. Zebedee's wife certainly had high ambition for her sons, as she requested that James and John would have special places at the Lord's side in His kingdom (Matthew 20:20-21).

John was one of the 'inner group' of the disciples along with Peter and James, who were taken into privileged situations such as the raising of Jairus's daughter (Mark 5:37) and the transfiguration (Mark 9:2). John was particularly close to the Lord and is usually identified as "the disciple whom Jesus loved" (John 13:23) and in John 21:20-24, the gospel writer confirms this. Their closeness is also confirmed by the fact that on the cross, Jesus committed His mother into the care of that disciple (John 19:26-27).

James and John were given the affectionate nickname *Boanerges* (= 'sons of thunder') by the Lord (Mark 3:17) possibly because they were boisterous and rough in their behaviour. Their inappropriate zeal is apparent in Luke 9:54 when they wanted to call down fire from heaven on a Samaritan village that did not welcome the Lord.

On the morning of the resurrection, it was John who ran with Peter to the tomb and believed when he saw the evidence of the grave clothes (John 20:8). In the days following Pentecost, John, along with Peter, emerges as one of the most prominent disciples (e.g. see Acts chapters 3 and 4) and Paul speaks of John as one of those "reputed to be pillars" in the Jerusalem church (Galatians 2:9). In Acts 8 we read that John and Peter were sent by the Jerusalem church to Samaria to enable the new converts there to receive the Holy Spirit (Acts 8:14-17). Thereafter, in Acts, there is little mention of John as the focus shifts to Paul and his ministry. It is not certain when John left Jerusalem but he appears to have been exiled on the island of Patmos, where he received the vision contained in the book of Revelation (Revelation 1:9-11).

The four gospel writers, then, were very different individuals:

- Matthew, a Jew who worked for the Roman occupying forces and who would be regarded as a traitor to his people. Yet he became one of the twelve and followed the Messiah, the fulfiller of Jewish expectations;

- Mark, a young man who observed the life of the Lord Jesus and the twelve disciples as they visited his mother's house and who subsequently went on to act as an assistant to both Peter and Paul;
- Luke, a Gentile doctor, educated, careful and observant, who travelled extensively with Paul. There is no indication that he was among the early disciples and he carefully researched the material for his gospel;
- John, the beloved disciple, closer to the Lord Jesus than any of the others, who wrote his gospel as an eyewitness account of the Lord's earthly ministry.

The diverse personalities of the four writers meant that their approaches to presenting the message of Jesus were also different – they had different styles and they had different audiences in mind. So, while they are all broadly describing the same events, their emphases are distinctive – some mention incidents not covered by the others, while there are telling omissions in different writers' accounts of the same events.

We will now discuss the aims of the four gospel writers and their intended readerships.

The aims of the gospel writers

Matthew

Matthew presents the Lord Jesus as the King of Israel, the fulfiller of Old Testament prophecy (e.g. 1:21-22; 2:15; 13:35; 21:4) and clearly has a Jewish audience in mind. He makes reference to the 'holy city' or the 'holy place' (4:5; 24:15; 27:53) and frequently mentions the Mosaic Law (e.g. 7:12; 23:23). It is Matthew who records the Lord's statement that "not the smallest letter, not the least stroke of a pen, will by any means disappear from the Law until everything is accomplished" (5:18). There are far more Old Testament references in Matthew than in any of the other gospels and he portrays the Lord as Israel's Messiah.

Matthew opens his gospel with a genealogy of the Lord Jesus (1:1-17) and he begins that genealogy by presenting Him as "the son of David, the son of Abraham" (1:1). When the Magi came to find Jesus, they came looking for "the one who has been born king of the Jews" (2:2). Herod knew whom they meant for he immediately summoned the chief priests and teachers to ask them "where the Christ was to be born" (2:4).

In Matthew's Gospel the Lord's ministry is clearly focused on Israel. The Lord tells the Canaanite woman, "I was sent only to the lost sheep of Israel" (15:24) and the disciples, when they are sent out on a missionary journey, are instructed:

> "Do not go among the Gentiles or enter any town of the Samaritans. Go rather to the lost sheep of Israel." (Matthew 10:5-6)

Graham Scroggie says:[3]

---

[3] W Graham Scroggie, *A Guide to the Gospels*, Pickering & Inglis, 1973, p248

> More than any other of the gospels, Matthew's is allied with the Hebrew Scriptures in theme and tone; their subjects are its subjects, the Messiah, Israel, The Law, the Kingdom and Prophecy. Jewish ideas and terms characterise the whole record.

Matthew's focus, then, is very much on the nation of Israel and he presents Jesus as the One of whom the prophets had spoken.

Mark

Mark's presentation of the Lord Jesus is as a servant. He is constantly in action and there is less in the way of discourse than there is in the other gospels. Mark begins his gospel abruptly with the words: "The beginning of the gospel about Jesus Christ, the Son of God" (Mark 1:1) and follows this with a quotation from Isaiah about John the Baptist as the preparer of the way for the Lord.

No extended genealogy of the Lord is provided; He is portrayed as a servant and a servant's genealogy is irrelevant. But the parentage of this Servant is given; He is 'the Son of God' (Mark 1:1). There is also no mention of His birth and childhood. Jesus is introduced to us in the first chapter when He comes to be baptised, calls the disciples and begins His teaching and healing ministry.

Mark is often regarded as a writer to the Romans and it is argued that the tone of action and service in the gospel would appeal to the Roman mind. Mark makes a curious comment in 15:21 that Simon of Cyrene was the father of Alexander and Rufus, as if he expects his readers to know these men. Rufus and his mother are mentioned as close friends of Paul in Romans 16:13 and appear to be prominent members of the church in Rome. Certainly it does appear that Mark's audience were not expected to be familiar with the land of Israel, or Jewish terms: Mark provides the meaning of *Boanerges* (3:17), *Talitha cumi* (5:41), *abba* (14:36) and other Aramaic words; he explains Jewish customs such as the practice of washing hands before eating (7:1-4); he also points out the geographical location of the Mount of Olives (13:3) and that the Jordan is a river (1:5).

However, the Roman church seems to have been comprised of both Jewish and Gentile believers and if Mark was writing for them he may have had a mixed audience in mind. This is not surprising if he had worked extensively with Peter, whose ministry was primarily to Jews (see Galatians 2:8), and also with Paul, the apostle to the Gentiles (Romans 11:13).

Luke

Luke was a Gentile writing to another Gentile (Theophilus) and he told him at the start of his gospel what he was aiming to achieve:

> Many have undertaken to draw up an account of the things that have been fulfilled among us, just as they were handed down to us by those who from the first were eyewitnesses and servants of the word. Therefore, since I myself have carefully investigated everything from the beginning, it seemed good also to me to write an orderly account for you, most excellent Theophilus, so that you may know the certainty of the things you have been taught. (Luke 1:1-4)

So Luke declares himself to be a careful researcher and this is apparent in the painstaking detail with which he presents historic information. For example:

> In those days Caesar Augustus issued a decree that a census should be taken of the entire Roman world. (This was the first census that took place while Quirinius was governor of Syria). (Luke 2:1-2)

> In the fifteenth year of the reign of Tiberius Caesar – when Pontius Pilate was governor of Judea, Herod tetrarch

> of Galilee, his brother Philip tetrarch of Iturea and Traconitis, and Lysanias tetrarch of Abilene – during the high priesthood of Annas and Caiphas, the word of God came ... (Luke 3:1-2)

His writing is scholarly and his message is directed to Theophilus and educated Greeks like him. As with Mark, he assumes that his readers are unfamiliar with Jewish practices and places: he explains that Capernaum is a city of Galilee (4:31), that the feast of unleavened bread is called the Passover (22:11) and that the village of Emmaus is about seven miles from Jerusalem (24:13). Luke also dates the Lord's birth and John's ministry by reference to the reigns of Roman emperors and governors. Since he is writing for Gentiles, Luke emphasises the wider scope of the Lord's ministry, highlighting God's care for the outsider (Luke 4:26-27).

Luke presents Jesus as the ideal man. Like Matthew, he provides the Lord's genealogy but he traces it back to Adam with no subdivisions at David or Abraham.

John

John was a Jewish writer and we know from Galatians 2:9 that he, along with Peter and James, agreed that they would concentrate their ministry on Jews, while Paul would focus on Gentiles. This emphasis is confirmed in John 20:30-31, where John explains the purpose of his gospel:

> Jesus did many other miraculous signs in the presence of his disciples, which are not recorded in this book. But these are written that you may believe that Jesus is the Christ, the Son of God, and that by believing you may have life in his name.

John's purpose is to present evidence to demonstrate that Jesus of Nazareth is the fulfiller of Jewish expectations – the Christ (Messiah), the Anointed One, whom it was predicted in the Old

Testament, would come to deliver His people Israel. Unlike Matthew and Luke, John does not include a genealogy of the Lord. In his opening verse John presents Him as God … so how could God have a genealogy? Instead, in the opening verse, he takes us back to the beginning of time to speak of the Word, who "was with God" and who "was God."

John's style of writing is different from the other three gospels. He is an eye-witness of the Lord's ministry and paints a personal picture of the Lord Jesus. Sometimes it is difficult to separate his own words from the Lord's (e.g. in John 3:5-21). The content of the gospel is also very different; of the eight miracles or "signs" included in John, six do not occur in the other gospels (the exceptions being the feeding of the five thousand and the walking on the water). How could it be so different? A number of writers have suggested that John had the other three gospels in front of him as he wrote. However, he used them, not to duplicate their content, but to fill in some of the blanks and present signs and incidents that he witnessed, which were not in the other gospel records. For example, John does not record the raising of Jairus's daughter. However, we know from Luke 8:51 that he was present at the event. John is therefore deliberately selective. As he himself says, the Lord did so many signs that, if they were all written down, the whole world would not have room for the books that would be written (John 21:25).

The differences between the four gospel records are summarised in the table opposite..

Table 1: The differences between the four gospel records

Theme	Matthew	Mark	Luke	John
The author	Jew; Tax collector; one of the twelve	Jew; Helper to Peter and Paul; social connection with Jesus and the twelve	Gentile; Medical doctor; helper to Paul; careful researcher	Jew; Fisherman; one of the twelve; the disciple whom Jesus loved
Readership	Israel	Romans	Greeks like Theophilus	Mainly Jews of the dispersion
Old Testament citations and allusions	128: one every 8.3 verses	63: one every 10.5 verses	96; one every 12 verses	43; one every 20.4 verses
Presentation of the Lord Jesus	King of the Jews	Servant	The Perfect Man	The Christ, the Son of God
Genealogy	Son of David, Son of Abraham	Son of God	Son of Adam	In the beginning was the Word ... the Word was God
Approach	Extensive use of Old Testament to show Jesus as Israel's Christ and king	Shows Christ in action, healing, teaching and travelling	Chronological approach; in his teaching and parables he shows the inclusion of the outsider	Uses signs, discourses, testimonies and teaching to show that Jesus is Christ

Section 2: Comparing the Gospels

Section 2: Comparing the Gospels

The central themes

One writer who attempted to compare the gospels was E W Bullinger. In the notes of his *Companion Bible* he states that the central themes of each of the gospels are the same.

Table 2: The central themes of the gospels

Theme	Matthew	Mark	Luke	John
The Kingdom proclaimed	4:12-7:29	1:14- 20	4:14b-5:11	1:35- 4:54
The King proclaimed	8:1-16:20	1:21- 8:30	5:12- 9:21	5:1- 6:71
The King rejected	16:21- 20:34	8:31-10:52	9:22-18:43	7:1-11:54a
The Kingdom rejected	21:1- 26:35	11:1-14:25	19:1- 22:38	11:54b-18:1

The Gospels do appear to be structured round these four themes, though we might not agree precisely with his divisions or the exact order of events. For example:

We have Christ introduced as the King of the Jews very early in Matthew (Matthew 2:2), before the proclamation of the kingdom

(Matthew 3:3; 4:17). Similarly in John: he is called King of Israel in John 1:49, but we do not hear of the kingdom until John 3:3. On the other hand, in Mark we hear of the kingdom in chapter 1 but there is no reference to Christ being king until chapter 15. In Luke it is similar, with early references to the kingdom in chapter 1 and 4, but no reference to Christ as king until chapter 19. So although one may not agree with Bullinger's division and order, he is correct to say that the proclamation of king and kingdom are the key features of the early parts of all four gospels.

When it comes to the rejections, opposition to Christ Himself built up first. In Matthew 9:3 the teachers of the law accuse Him of blasphemy and in Matthew 9:34 the Pharisees stated that Christ cast out demons "by the prince of demons". Then they charged Him of breaking the Law of Moses (Matthew 12:2) and accused Him of performing His miracles by the power of Beelzebub (Matthew 12:24). It is not surprising, then, that after that Christ called them "A wicked and adulterous generation" (Matthew 12:39).

At a certain point in His ministry, the Lord reveals that He will be rejected by the Jewish leaders and killed. From that point on, He concentrates His teaching on His disciples, rather than on the people as a whole. Much of the teaching to His disciples was done in parables[4] because "the knowledge of the secrets of the kingdom of heaven have been given to you (the disciples) but not

---

[4] Parables actually hide truth rather than make truth easier to understand. More on this, and other aspects of parables, can be found in the book *The Purpose of Parables* by Michael Penny and published by The Open Bible Trust. See also the YouTube video *Learning from Preposterous Parables* by Michael Penny published by the Christian Resources Exhibition.

to them" (Matthew 13:11). We will find this same scenario in each of the gospels.
Shortly after he started to teach in parables, He told the Twelve that He was to "be *rejected* by the elders, chief priests and teachers of the law" (Mark 8:31; see also Matthew 16:21; Luke 9:22), and described Himself as the stone the builders *rejected* (Matthew 21:42; Mark 12:10; Luke 20:17).

Caiaphas stated that "it is better for you that one man die for the people than that the whole nation perish", showing his preference to a life in the Roman Empire to one in the Kingdom of God (John 11:50). And, in the words of the parable, the subjects said, "We don't want this man to be our king" (Luke 19:14), a theme that runs through other parables. Thus we see both the King and the kingdom being rejected.

The section on rejection ends with His crucifixion and burial. Finally, in the closing chapter of the first three gospels and the closing two chapters of John's Gospel, we have the account of the resurrection and the appearances to His disciples.

As we study the gospels we see these four major themes in them all. All four commence with either a statement about Christ as King or with comments on the Kingdom. However, as we progress through we find that both He (and His teachings) and the Kingdom are rejected. This rejection gets stronger as we progress through the gospels. It came to a head after a little over three years. He rode into Jerusalem on a donkey and the days following saw intense conflict resulting, in the end, in His arrest, trials and crucifixion. That, so the authorities thought, would be the end of the matter … but they were wrong.

We will next consider the common central themes in more detail.

The preparation for the proclamation

There are three sections in each of the four gospels that serve as preparatory material to introduce us to the proclamation of the king and the kingdom – the lineage of the Lord Jesus Christ, the ministry of John the Baptist pointing to Him, and the Lord's baptism which is a commissioning of Him for His ministry.

At the start of each of the gospels, we have a lineage of the Lord. In Matthew it is an extensive genealogy, showing Christ to be both the Son of David and the Son of Abraham – the correct credentials for one to be King of the Jews (Matthew 1:1-17).

Luke's lineage is another extensive genealogy, not only going through David and Abraham, but going further, showing Him to be both the 'son of Adam' and the 'son of God' (Luke 3:23-38). These were the right credentials for the One who was to be the kinsman redeemer of all humanity.

Mark's lineage is the shortest. He quite simply states that Jesus Christ is "the Son of God" (Mark 1:1). And in stating this he is very much in line with John's lineage. There we read:

> In the beginning was the Word, and the Word was with God, and the Word was God. (John 1:1)

Here John clearly states that Jesus, the Word, was God … yet in Mark we read He was "the Son of God". Is there a difference? Some may say 'yes', but in essence the answer is 'no'. We, as Gentiles, may struggle with this, thinking that the 'Son of God' cannot possibly be 'God'. However, at the start of his gospel John states that Jesus is God and towards the end declares that he wrote his gospel to demonstrate that Jesus is "the Son of God." (John 20:31). Thus to this Jew the 'Son of God' was 'God' and John's view of the Lord's lineage is thus consistent with that of Mark and the other gospels.

John the Baptist appears early in all four gospels; he was the forerunner, who had come to prepare the way for the Lord (Matthew 3:3; Mark 1:3; Luke 3:4; John 1:23). He baptised the people, predicting the coming of Christ, who was greater than him and who would baptise them with the Holy Spirit (Matthew 3:11-12; Mark 1:8; Luke 3:16; John 1:33). In fact, he pointed the Lord Jesus out to his disciples as:

> ... the Lamb of God, who takes away the sin of the world! (John 1:29)

His message to the people was that they should repent because the kingdom of heaven and the time of judgment are near (Matthew 3:2; Luke 3:9, 17). The reason for John's ministry was in order that the Lord Jesus would be revealed to Israel (John 1:31).

All four gospels record Jesus' baptism by John in the Jordan and the Spirit coming down on Him in the form of a dove. This identified Him to John as the Son of God (John 1:34). This was further confirmed by the voice of God saying:

> This is my Son, whom I love; with him I am well pleased. (Matthew 3:17; Mark 1:11; Luke 3:22)

The parallel passages for this section are shown in Table 3 below.

Table 3: The Preparation for the Proclamation

Subject	Matthew	Mark	Luke	John
Christ's lineage	1:1-17	1:1	3:23-38	1:1
John the Baptist	3:1-12	1:2-8	3:1-20	1:6-28
Christ's baptism	3:13-17	1:9-11	3:21-22	1:29-34

The King and the Kingdom proclaimed

Jesus' ministry commenced when John the Baptist was put in prison (Matthew 4:12; Mark 1:14; Luke 3:20) and the message He preached was similar to that of John:

> Repent, for the kingdom of heaven is near. (Matthew 4:17)

The Lord thus came proclaiming the closeness of the kingdom. The potential for the establishment of the kingdom had never been greater – the time was ripe for the people of Israel because the king was among them. Would they recognise Him or reject Him?

All three synoptic gospels reveal the Lord performing miracles, teaching the people how they should live and proclaiming that the kingdom was near. A recurring comment from those who heard Him was a recognition of His authority – in His teaching (Matthew 7:28-29; Mark 1:22; Luke 4:32) and His power over evil spirits (Mark 1:27; Luke 4:36).
The teaching and the miracles were His credentials as the Messiah of Israel.

Similarly, John structures his coverage of Jesus' ministry round a series of signs and discourses with the Pharisees, with the express purpose that his readers might believe that "Jesus is the Christ (the Messiah), the Son of God" (John 20:31).

John also describes how many of the people whom Jesus encountered during His ministry gave testimony to His identity. For example:

- John the Baptist: "I have seen and testified that this is the Son of God" (John 1:34)
- Nathanael: "Rabbi, you are the Son of God; you are the king of Israel" (John 1:49)
- The woman at the well: "Could this be the Christ?" (John 4:29).
- The Samaritans: "We know that this man really is the Saviour of the world" (John 4:42)
- The crowd, following the feeding of the five thousand: "Surely this is the Prophet who is to come into the world" (John 6:14)
- The man born blind: "Lord I believe," and he worshipped him (John 9:38)

The Lord was supported in His ministry by His disciples and others. The gospels record the calling of the disciples (Matthew 4; Mark 1; Luke 5; John 1). Later the Lord sent them out to preach the same message that He had been preaching:

> As you go, preach this message: 'The kingdom of heaven is near.' Heal the sick, raise the dead, cleanse those who have leprosy, drive out demons. (Matthew 10:7-8; see also Mark 6:12-13; Luke 9:1-2)

Yet it is clear that His message was not being completely accepted. Although many of the people followed Him and listened to His every word, they were uncertain about whether He was the Christ or not. This ambivalence is spelled out in detail in John 7:25-31.

The Jewish leaders, however, opposed Him from the start. Increasingly, He condemned the nation, and its leaders in particular, for their unbelief. We find this in all four gospels – Matthew 11:20-24; 12:38-45; Mark 6:1-6; Luke 11:37-54; John 8:31-47.

There was a point in the Lord's ministry where He started to reveal that His proclamation of the coming kingdom to Israel would not be a success. The first sign of the change was when He started to teach by parables. In Matthew 13:1-9, Mark 4:1-9 and Luke 8:4-8 we find the parable of the sower and the disciples immediately asked why He was using this form of teaching. His reply indicated that He was doing so to make the truth known only to a select few:

> 'The knowledge of the secrets of the kingdom of heaven has been given to you, but not to them ... That is why I speak to them in parables. (Matthew 13:11, 13. See also Mark 4:10-11 and Luke 8:9-10)

We often think of the parables as being stories to enable people to understand more clearly; in fact, they were designed to hide the truth from many of those who listened. The Lord's ministry had changed and He was starting to instruct those who had put their faith in Him.

In Matthew 16:16, we have Peter's confession of Jesus as 'the Christ, the Son of the living God' and five verses later we read that:

> From that time on Jesus began to explain to his disciples that he must go to Jerusalem and suffer many things at the hands of the elders, chief priests and teachers of the law,

> and that he must be killed and on the third day be raised to life. (Matthew 16:21)

The newness of this teaching is evidenced by the fact that Peter immediately rebuked Him and denied that this would happen (Matthew 16:22). The gospel of the kingdom, preached earlier by the twelve disciples could therefore not have contained any reference to the Lord's death.

We find a similar pattern in Mark 8:27-32 and Luke 9:18-22. In John's Gospel the raising of Lazarus was the last straw for the Jewish leaders and thereafter they plotted to take the Lord's life (John 11:53). John concludes:

> Therefore Jesus no longer moved about publicly among the Jews. Instead he withdrew to a region near the desert, to a village called Ephraim, where he stayed with his disciples. (John 11:54)

The tipping point had been reached. The Lord's task was now to prepare the disciples for His death and what was to follow.

Table 4: The King and the Kingdom proclaimed

Subject	Matthew	Mark	Luke	John
Christ's message	4:17	1:15	4:18-19	3:16-21
The calling of the disciples	4:18-22	1:16-20	5:1-11; 27-28	1:35-51
Miracles and teaching	4:23-16:12	1:21-8:26	4:14-9:17	2:1-12:19
The parables of proclamation	13:1-15:20	4:1-34	8:1-8	-
Condemnation of the Jews	11:20-24; 12:38-45	6:1-6	11:37-54	8:31-47
The Lord predicts His death	16:21-23	8:31-33	9:22	12:20

The King and the Kingdom rejected

Immediately after the Lord revealed to His disciples that He was going to be put to death, we have the incident of the transfiguration (Matthew 17:1-13; Mark 9:2-13; Luke 9:28-36). Here Peter, James and John were given a glimpse of the glorified Lord Jesus and heard God's voice confirming His identity as God's son, just as they had heard it at His baptism. This confirmation re-enforced their faith for the difficult days that lay ahead.

Thereafter, Jesus' teaching to His disciples took on a tone of urgency: many of the earlier parables in Matthew 13, Mark 4 and Luke 8 had been about the proclamation of the message, e.g. the sower, the mustard seed, lamp on a stand, the hidden treasure and the pearl of great price. Now the parables were more about accountability, repentance and judgment. For example:

- The unmerciful servant (Matthew 18)
- The workers in the vineyard (Matthew 20)
- The two sons and the tenants (Matthew 21; Mark 12; Luke 20)
- The wedding banquet (Matthew 22; Luke 14)
- The ten virgins and the talents (Matthew 25)
- The rich fool (Luke 12)
- The lost sheep, coin and son (Matthew 18; Luke 15)
- The ten minas (Luke 19)
- The fig tree (Luke 21)
- The rich man and Lazarus (Luke 16)

Although the Lord continued to engage in debate with the Pharisees and crowds of people still followed Him for healing and teaching, His main focus shifted to His disciples as He concentrated increasingly on instructing them. The message was that they were to be prepared for the Lord to return at the end of the age, which could be at any time. The parables about the servants, the tenants, the virgins and the wedding banquet all illustrated the need for His followers to be living appropriately when He returned. In Matthew 24, Mark 13 and Luke 17 and 21 the Lord gave specific teaching about the end of the age and the signs that would precede it, so that, although only the Father knew when it would happen, they would be able to read the signs and be ready.

In John 14-17 we have four chapters in which the Lord privately instructed His disciples to prepare them for His departure. That section ends with the Lord praying not only for the eleven disciples, but for all who would believe as a result of their message.

As the time for end of His ministry neared, the Lord seems to have made one final attempt to convince the people that He was the Messiah by riding into Jerusalem on a donkey. Matthew 21:4 tells us that this was done 'to fulfil what was spoken through the prophet,' indicating the Lord's purpose. The people appeared to have understood to some extent because they went ahead of Him shouting 'Hosannah to the Son of David' (Matthew 21:9). From there, He went into the temple area and drove out the moneychangers. But the chief priests and teachers of the law were scandalised:

> "Do you hear what these children are saying?" they asked him.

> “Yes,” replied Jesus, “have you never read, ‘From the lips of children and infants you have ordained praise.’” (Matthew 21:16)

These incidents occur in all four gospels (see also Mark 11; Luke 19; John 2 and 12) showing their importance. However Matthew and Mark follow these events with a small but significant episode where the Lord, not finding fruit on a fig tree, curses the tree, which withers the next day (Matthew21; Mark 11). This petty vindictiveness appears out of character with the Lord Jesus but the fig tree had long been seen as a symbol of Israel. In Matthew 24:32, Jesus told His disciples that they should look to the condition of the "fig tree" for evidence of the nearness of the coming of the Son of Man. In Luke 13:6-9 Jesus told a parable of a man who planted a fig tree and came looking for fruit. Finding none, he instructs his gardener to cut it down. The gardener, however, argues that the tree should be given a further chance and gains a year’s reprieve. By the time we reach Luke 19, however, the rejection of the Lord by the Jewish leaders had become entrenched. There would be no reprieve this time.

As the Lord’s ministry neared its climax, Matthew 26, Mark 14 and John 12 all record the very symbolic incident of the Lord having His feet anointed by Mary at Bethany. In all three accounts the Lord pointed out the significance of this incident. For example:

> When she poured this perfume on my body, she did it to prepare me for burial (Matthew 26:12)

The Lord’s ministry was now nearing its close and the gospels go on to record the events which bring them all to their climax.

Table 5: The King and the Kingdom rejected

Subject	Matthew	Mark	Luke	John
The transfiguration	17:1-13	9:2-13	9:28-36	-
The parables of accountability	18:10-25:46	12:1-12	12:13-21:36	-
The signs of the end of the age	24:1-25:46	13:1-37	17:20-37; 21:5-36	-
The ride into Jerusalem	21:1-11	11:1-11	19:28-44	12:12-19
Cleansing the temple	21:12-17	11:12-19	19:45-47	2:13-25
The Lord anointed at Bethany	26:6-13	14:1-10	-	12:1-11

The Climax of the Gospels

Having written about who Jesus is, what He did and taught, and what happened to Him, all four writers converge on the Passover meal. John alone does ***not*** mention the bread and wine or anything to do with the New Covenant. However, in chapter 6 he has already introduced the concept of believers "eating" the Lord's flesh and "drinking" His blood as a symbol of of believing in Him (v 35,53-54), showing their identification with Him.
There were two critical events at that meal: the identification of Judas as the betrayer and the Lord's prediction of Peter's denials. Matthew, Mark and John describe in some detail how the Lord points out Judas as the traitor. John describes the conversation between Peter and the disciple whom Jesus loved (John himself) to identify Judas. The whole episode must have happened very quickly since none of the disciples appears to have attempted to prevent Judas from leaving. Luke's account of the incident is the shortest and makes no mention of Judas, although at the start of chapter 22 Luke reports Judas's meeting with the chief priests.

All four gospels record the Lord's prediction of Peter's denials. Peter was destined to be one of the leaders of the fledgling church in Jerusalem but before that he had to be tested beyond his limits. Luke 22:31-32 shows that Satan appears to have been given permission to sift Peter like wheat. The traumatic experience that Peter was to go through was to be part of his maturing process and perhaps helped to teach him not to rely on himself.

Table 6: The Passover Meal

Subject	Matthew	Mark	Luke	John
The Meal itself	26:17-30	14:12-26	22:7-30	13:2-17:26 (?)
Interaction with Judas	26:20-25	14:17-22	22:22-23	13:18-30
Prediction of Peter's denials	26:31-35	14:27-31	22:31-34	13:37-38

Following the meal the Lord and the eleven disciples moved out into the Garden of Gethsemane. All four gospels refer to the garden, but John only mentions it very briefly and omits reference to the Lord's agony at what lay before Him. Some have argued that John, focusing on Jesus' deity, did not wish to report anything that suggested human frailty.

The arrival of Judas and the Lord's arrest are given by all four gospels in varying amounts of detail. They all record Peter's assault on Malchus, the high priest's servant but only John 18:10 names Peter as the attacker. Matthew, Mark and Luke describe how Judas kissed the Lord to identify Him, while John makes no reference to the kiss. Mark alone mentions the young man, hiding in the garden who escaped naked when he was discovered, prompting some commentators to suggest that the young man was Mark himself.

When the Lord was brought before the Sanhedrin for interrogation He was asked a variety of questions. Matthew, Mark and Luke all report the Lord stating explicitly that He was the Son of God, while John, rather surprisingly, does not mention this. However, John gives much more detail than the others of the

Lord's interaction with Pilate, in which the Lord states that His kingdom "is not of this world" (John 18:36).

Table 7: The Lord's arrest

Event	Matthew	Mark	Luke	John
The garden	26:36-46	14:32-42	22:39-46	18:1
Arrival of Judas	26:47-49	14:43-45	22:47-48	18:2-11
The arrest	26:50-56	14:46-52	22:49-54	18:12
The Sanhedrin	26:57-68	14:53-65	22:54; 22:66-71	18:13-14; 18:19-24
Peter's denials	26:69-75	14:66-72	22:55-62	18:15-17; 18:25-27;
Before Pilate	27:11-26	15:1-15	23:1-25	18:28-19:16

The four gospels describe the Lord's crucifixion, death and burial in variable detail, before going on to record His glorious resurrection.

At the crucifixion, Matthew and Mark record that both robbers crucified with the Lord insulted Him. John mentions the two robbers but does not report that they spoke. Only Luke, the champion of the outsider, says that one of them repented and was promised a place with the Lord in Paradise (Luke 23:43). All the gospels mention that the Lord was offered wine vinegar to drink, but only John explains that this was in response to the Lord's complaint that He was thirsty.

The Lord's death was accompanied by strange signs. Matthew, Mark and Luke say that the curtain of the temple was torn from top to bottom and Matthew describes an earthquake and that many holy people came out of their graves (Matthew 27:51-54). John uniquely describes the Lord commissioning him to look after His mother. He also refers to the soldiers gambling for the Lord's clothes and to them not breaking His legs as being in fulfilment of Old Testament prophecy.

After the Lord died, Joseph of Arimathea acquired His body from Pilate and buried Him in his own tomb, watched by Mary Magdalene and Mary the mother of James. John does not mention the women but states that Joseph was accompanied by Nicodemus (John 19:39-42).

There are also minor differences between the gospels' account of the resurrection. Matthew describes the angel who rolled away the stone and the terror of the guards. He also explains that the guards were subsequently bribed to say that the disciples had stolen the Lord's body (Matthew 28:11-15). Matthew, Mark and Luke report the angel's encouraging words to the women. John only mentions Mary Magdalene going to the tomb and, finding it empty, rushing to tell Peter and John what she has found. They run to the tomb and confirm what Mary had said. In Luke, Peter runs to the tomb to confirm the women's report.

Table 8: The Lord's death, burial and resurrection

Event	Matthew	Mark	Luke	John
Crucifixion	27:32-44	15:21-32	23:26-43	19:17-27
Death	27:45-56	15:33-41	23:44-49	19:28-37
Burial	27:57-61	15:42-47	23:50-56	19:38-42
Resurrection	28:1-10	16:1-8	24:1-12	20:1-9

The Lord appeared to a number of His followers after the resurrection and these are recorded in the four gospels. He appeared to the women first and then, subsequently to the disciples. Not all of the appearances are recorded in all the gospels, but they all record one or more of these appearances.

In Matthew the Lord appeared to the two Marys immediately after they visited the tomb. John gives a detailed and heart-warming account of Mary Magdalene meeting the Lord in the garden after Peter and John have gone home from the empty tomb. This meeting is also referred to in Mark. Mark and Luke (in more detail) both record the Lord's meeting with the two disciples on the Emmaus road, and Luke and John describe a meeting with the disciples in Jerusalem. Luke alone mentions a meeting with Peter.

The first three gospels describe the Lord meeting with His disciples to give them their great commission to go into the world (Matthew 28:19-20; Mark 16:15-16) and to be witnesses (Luke 24:48) immediately prior to His ascension. John does not mention this incident but instead relates an episode where the disciples, instructed by the Lord, make a miraculous catch of fish. In the subsequent meeting on the beach, the Lord re-instates Peter and commissions him to "feed my sheep."

Table 9: The resurrection appearances

Appearances	Matthew	Mark	Luke	John
To Mary		16:9-11		20:10-18
To the women	28:8-10			
To the two		16:12-13	24:13-32	
To Peter			24:34	
To the disciples in Jerusalem			24:35-45	20:19-23
To Thomas				20:24-29
To the Eleven		16:14		
To the disciples in Galilee	28:16-17			21:1-14

These are the themes which are common to all four gospels. However, there are two topics that require some separate consideration – the Lord's Miracles and the titles that were given to the Lord in the gospels

The Lord's miracles

We do not need to be great students of the Bible to know that all four gospels record many of the miracles that Jesus performed. The miracles fall generally into two types: miracles over nature and miracles of healing. All four gospels record examples of these.

Miracles over nature include the feeding of 5,000 and Christ walking on water, which are common to all four gospels. Others include calming the storm, feeding 4,000, cursing the fig tree and turning water into wine.

Healing miracles abound, although none are common to all four gospels. In some places in the Synoptics it simply states that Jesus healed "every disease and sickness" (Matthew 4:23). However, there are a considerable number of healings described in detail and the majority of those fall into four categories: namely healing the blind, the lame, the deaf and the dumb. The reason for this is that these miracles were more than miracles.

John rightly calls them miraculous 'signs'. Such healing miracles were not only acts of compassion and power; they 'signified' something. They signified that "Jesus is the Christ[5], the Son of God" (John 20:31). This may not be obvious to Gentiles living in the 21st Century, but to 1st Century Jews, who knew their (Old Testament) Scriptures, the miracles of healings should have spoken volumes. The Old Testament prophesied the following:

---

[5] Although we today use 'Christ' as a name for Jesus it is the Greek equivalent of 'Messiah'. Thus John was writing to prove that "Jesus is the Messiah, the Son of God".

> "Be strong, do not fear; your God will come, he will come with vengeance; with divine retribution. He will come to save you." Then will the eyes of the blind be opened and the ears of the deaf unstopped. Then will the lame leap like a deer, and the mute tongue shout for joy."(Isaiah 35:4-6)

So when God came to save them … then, at that time, "will the eyes of the blind be opened and the ears of the deaf unstopped". Then, at that time, when your God comes to save you, "will the lame leap like a deer and the mute tongue shout for joy."
It is true that Jesus did other healing miracles, such as curing leprosy and healing the woman with an issue of blood, but the healings of the blind and deaf, the lame and dumb, were the ones the gospel writers mentioned more than others.

When John the Baptist was in prison, he sent his disciples to ask Jesus, "Are you the one who was to come, or should we expect someone else?" (Matthew 11:3). It is interesting to note that Christ did not give a straight answer to this but replied,

> "Go back and report to John what you hear and see: The blind receive sight, the lame walk, those with leprosy are cured, the deaf hear, the dead are raised, and the good news is preached to the poor." (Matthew 11:4-5)

These miracles, especially those prophesied in Isaiah, showed that 'God' had come to save them. In John, they signified Jesus was the 'Son of God'. Thus the gospels show that the Son of God is Emmanuel, God with us … upon this earth.

The Lord's titles

There are various titles of the Lord Jesus Christ that all the gospel writers use a number of times. Consider the following titles and the frequency with which they occur in each gospel.

Table 10: The Lord's titles

Title	Matthew	Mark	Luke	John
King (of the Jews /Israel)	5	6	3	8
Son of God	8	2	6	8
Son of Man	31	14	25	12
Christ	17	7	13	21

Although each writer may have had a preferred title, each writer uses all four titles[6]. In fact all four of these titles can imply deity. Consider, for example, 'Son of Man'.

> For as lightning that comes from the east is visible even in the west, so will be the coming of the Son of Man ... At that time the sign of the Son of Man will appear in the sky, and all the nations of the earth will mourn. They will see the Son of Man coming on the clouds of the sky, with power and great glory. And he will send his angels with a loud trumpet call, and they will gather his elect from the four winds, from one end of the heavens to the other." (Matthew 24:27,30-31)

[6] The figures in Table 10 are taken from Wigram's *Englishman's Greek Concordance.*

Some today are reluctant to see the title "Son of Man" as referring to deity, but the high priest had no doubt in his mind and accused Christ of blasphemy.

> The high priest said to him, "I charge you under oath by the living God: Tell us if you are the Christ, the Son of God." "Yes, it is as you say," Jesus replied. "But I say to all of you: In the future you will see the Son of Man sitting at the right hand of the Mighty One and coming on the clouds of heaven." Then the high priest tore his clothes and said, "He has spoken blasphemy! Why do we need any more witnesses? Look, now you have heard the blasphemy. What do you think?" "He is worthy of death," they answered. (Matthew 26:63-66)

The high priest, and accusers, knew that Daniel had used this title.

> "In my vision at night I looked, and there before me was one like a son of man, coming with the clouds of heaven. He approached the Ancient of Days and was led into his presence. He was given authority, glory and sovereign power; all peoples, nations and men of every language worshipped him. His dominion is an everlasting dominion that will not pass away, and his kingdom is one that will never be destroyed." (Daniel 7:13-14)

Thus we can see that these titles … the Christ (Messiah), the Son of God and the Son of Man … indicate that Jesus is God incarnate … a theme each of the gospels has in common.

Similarly, titles such as the King of the Jews or the King of Israel. These are common to all four gospels and they, again, imply deity. For example, The Magi ask "Where is the one who has been born King of the Jews?" (Matthew 2:2). When Herod heard this he was troubled and enquired of the chief priests and teachers of the law "where the Christ (Messiah) was to be born" (Matthew 3:4). And Nathaniel declared, "You are the Son of God; you are the King of Israel" (John 1:49)

The prophet said of Him that "He will reign on David's throne and over his kingdom" (Isaiah 9:7). And this is exactly what the angel told Mary. He said of the child she was to bear that "The Lord God will give him the throne of his father David, and will reign over the house of Jacob for ever (Luke 1:32-33). All four gospels refer to Jesus as this King.

So far we have compared the gospels with one another, showing the common themes and demonstrating that, although there were some differences in approach, they were essentially proclaiming the same message – the Lord Jesus came to earth to proclaim the good news of the kingdom and to declare that the establishment of the kingdom was an imminent possibility, if they would accept Him as their Messiah. At some point during His ministry, the Lord revealed to His disciples that He would not be accepted by the people at this time and would be betrayed, tried and executed. However, three days later He would rise from the dead. All four gospels show Jesus preparing His disciples for these events and what would follow. The Lord's predictions were accurate and the gospels tell us of the events surrounding His execution. However, that was not the end and His resurrection was also described by all four gospel writers.

However, there are significant differences in emphasis between the gospel writers and in the following section we will explore these differences. For example, there are subtle differences in the way the different writers approach common incidents, each giving a slant appropriate to his purpose in writing. Some gospels include particular incidents which are omitted from others. The gospel of John is unique in its approach and the different aspects of that uniqueness will also be addressed.

Section 3: Contrasting the Gospels

Section 3: Contrasting the Gospels

Contrasts in common incidents in the synoptic gospels

As we discussed earlier in the booklet, the four writers had different aims and were not all writing with the same audience in mind. It is therefore interesting to note that there are a number of incidents recorded in more than one gospel, where there are differences in the emphases of the writers. The principal incidents are:

The Canaanite woman

In Matthew 15 we find a detailed account of a Canaanite woman who came to Jesus, seeking deliverance for her daughter from demon-possession. She addressed Him as "Lord, Son of David" (verse 22) and Jesus did not answer her. When the disciples complained that she was making a nuisance of herself He responded by saying:

> "I was sent only to the lost sheep of Israel." (verse 24)

The woman then engaged Him in conversation. Jesus was still not encouraging, telling her:

> "It is not right to take the children's bread and toss it to their dogs." (verse 26)

Her response to this was to claim entitlement to the crumbs that fall from the master's table, and on this basis, Jesus healed her daughter (verses 27-28).

Matthew, writing to Jews, emphasised the narrow focus on the Lord's ministry. He was Israel's king; He was Israel's Messiah. Therefore He was concentrating on them and any blessings that extended to outsiders were 'crumbs from the master's table.'

The encounter with the woman is not mentioned in Luke or John but Mark, who is writing to Gentiles, deals with it in chapter 7. Mark does not mention the Lord's statement that He was only sent to the lost sheep of Israel but he also makes a statement about the children's bread, which Matthew does not. This gives the woman the opportunity to claim the crumbs:

> *"First,* let the children eat all they want," he told her, "for it is not right to take the children's bread and toss it to their dogs." (verse 27)

So Mark also recognises the priority of Israel but points out the fact that Gentiles could still be blessed.

Riding into Jerusalem on a donkey

Matthew 21 describes the Lord riding into Jerusalem in fulfilment of prophecy, as Israel's king:

> This took place to fulfil what was spoken through the prophet: "Say to the Daughter of Zion, 'See, your king comes to you, gentle and riding on a donkey, on a colt, the foal of a donkey'"... The crowds that went ahead of him and those that followed shouted, "Hosannah to the Son of

> David! Blessed is he who comes in the name of the Lord!" (Matthew 21:4-5,9)

Luke greatly simplifies the events. Writing to a Gentile he says nothing about fulfilment of prophecy, or the fact that He is king of Zion or the Son of David, but simply says that He is 'the king who comes in the name of the Lord.'

> When he came near the place where the road goes down the Mount of Olives, the whole crowd of disciples began joyfully to praise God in loud voices for all the miracles they had seen: "Blessed is the king who comes in the name of the Lord! Peace in heaven and glory in the highest!" (Luke 19:37-38)

John the Baptist prophesied

Both Matthew and Luke quote from Isaiah 40 as they introduce John the Baptist as a forerunner of the Lord. Matthew quotes the prophecy briefly, whereas Luke gives the quotation in full since it goes on to state that not just Israel, but 'all mankind' will see the salvation of God.

> This is he who was spoken of through the prophet Isaiah: "A voice of one calling in the desert, 'Prepare the way for the Lord, make straight paths for him.'" (Matthew 3:3)

> As is written in the book of the words of Isaiah the prophet: "A voice of one calling in the desert, 'Prepare the way for the Lord, make straight paths for him. Every valley shall be filled in, every mountain and hill made low. The crooked roads shall become straight, the rough

> ways smooth. And all mankind will see God's salvation.'" (Luke 3:4-6)

The mission of the disciples

In Matthew 10, the Lord sent out the disciples on a preaching tour. However, He warned them that they were to limit their work to Jews only:

> These twelve Jesus sent out with the following instructions: "Do not go among the Gentiles or enter any town of the Samaritans. Go rather to the lost sheep of Israel. As you go, preach this message: 'The kingdom of heaven is near.' Heal the sick, raise the dead, cleanse those who have leprosy, drive out demons ..." (Matthew 10:5-8)

When Luke describes the same mission, he does not mention the restrictions that they were not to go to the Gentiles or the Samaritans:

> When Jesus had called the twelve together, he gave them power and authority to drive out all demons and to cure diseases, and he sent them out to preach the kingdom of God and to heal the sick. (Luke 9:1-2)

Mark also does not mention the restrictions:

> Calling the Twelve to him, he sent them out two by two and gave them authority over evil spirits ... They went out and preached that people should repent. They drove out many demons and anointed many sick people with oil and healed them. (Mark 6:7, 12)

Rejection at Nazareth

In Matthew 13:53-58 and Mark 6:1-6, there are brief sections dealing with Jesus' teaching in the synagogue at Nazareth. The two narratives are very similar in wording and style and appear to be describing the same incident. The people, hearing the Lord's teaching, are amazed, wondering about the source of his powers. However, they "took offence" at Him because He was the carpenter's son and they knew His family. The incident ends with the Lord's observation that a prophet is honoured everywhere but His home town, and both writers comment that He could do no miracles there because of their lack of faith (Matthew 13:58; Mark 6:5)

However, in Luke 4:16-30 there is a much longer narrative which shows similar exchanges to Matthew and Mark but also includes the Lord's statement that:

> "I assure you that there were many widows in Israel in Elijah's time ... Yet Elijah was not sent to any of them but to a widow in Zarephath in the region of Sidon. And there were many in Israel with leprosy in the time of Elisha the prophet, yet not one of them was cleansed – only Naaman the Syrian." (Luke 4:25-27)

In Luke's Gospel it is Christ's reference to Gentiles who were blessed in Old Testament times that arouses the anger of the people, rather than the mere fact that He is 'Joseph's son.' It is possible that these are different incidents but it is unlikely, given the similarities of the reactions of the congregation. Luke, writing chronologically, places the event fairly early in Jesus' ministry, when His work would be relatively unknown so it is understandable that the people of Nazareth were not aware of His reputation. However, if these are different incidents, this demonstrates the point that Luke records unique incidents to show the acceptance of Gentiles into God's blessings.

Luke, then, particularly emphasises the inclusion of Gentiles in the Lord's blessings. But there are a number of incidents that are unique to Luke, which highlight the way in which the Lord Jesus welcomes and blesses those members of Jewish society, who might be regarded as outcasts or rejects.

Luke's emphasis on the outsider

Luke was a close companion of Paul, the apostle to the Gentiles, and Luke also addresses a Gentile audience in his gospel. He wants to demonstrate that, although the Lord's earthly ministry was primarily to Israel, Gentiles were by no means excluded from future blessing. We have already seen the different emphases that Luke gives to incidents that are also included in Matthew's Gospel but in addition to these Luke brings in other incidents (parables and miracles) that are not mentioned in the other gospels. Luke also provides examples of situations where Jesus blesses someone who, though not a Gentile, would be considered an 'outsider' in Jewish society. In this section we will consider some of these.

The thief on the cross

All four gospels record that two others were crucified with the Lord. John says nothing of an interaction between them, while Matthew and Mark each report that both robbers abused Him. It is Luke alone who records the change of heart of one of the thieves, who, while admitting his crimes, asks the Lord to remember him when He comes into His kingdom. The Lord's reply showed that he had been accepted, even as his life ebbed away:

> Jesus answered him, "I tell you the truth, today you will be with me in paradise." (Luke 23:43)

The announcement of the Lord's birth to the shepherds

When the Lord was born in Bethlehem, Matthew tells of the Magi – who came from the east to Jerusalem to seek "the one who has been born king of the Jews" (Matthew 2:2). They were important people and brought expensive gifts fit for a king. Appropriately, they went to Herod in Jerusalem initially, but were redirected to Bethlehem where they found the infant Jesus. This must have taken some considerable time and it could have been almost 2 years after His birth because Herod ordered the killing of all boys in Bethlehem two years old and under (Matthew 2:16).

Luke says nothing of the Magi but relates how the birth of Jesus was announced to common shepherds on the hillsides around Bethlehem. These were the first to go and see the baby lying in the manger (Luke 2:16). They had no gifts to bring, but as they returned to their flocks, they rejoiced and praised God for what they had seen (Luke 2:20).

Blessings on Samaritans

Luke is the only gospel to record the parable of the good Samaritan, told by the Lord in Luke 10 in answer to the question "who is my neighbour?" The Samaritan is praised for helping the injured Jew, in contrast to the priest and the Levite who 'pass by on the other side.'

In Luke 17:11-19 we read of ten lepers who were healed by the Lord but only one of them returned to thank Him – and he was a Samaritan. The Lord blesses him with the words "your faith has made you well" (Luke 17:19). The word translated 'made well' in this passage is usually translated 'saved,' and this shows that faith that results in deliverance was not the prerogative of the Jews.

Blessings on outsiders

There are several incidents in Luke where those on the margins of Jewish society were blessed, sometimes to the exclusion of the privileged:

Luke 15:11-32 sets out the parable of the prodigal son. The profligate younger son is welcomed back into the fold while the 'good' older son is shown in a very bad light, as he refuses to welcome his brother home. Many have inferred that Jesus was referring to the Pharisees in the character of the elder son because of their negative attitude to 'tax collectors and sinners.'

In Luke 16:19-31, we find the parable of the rich man and Lazarus. Here we have a 'role reversal' where the rich man, who does not seem to have been particularly evil – he allowed Lazarus to eat the crumbs from his table, after all – is condemned to hell (*hades*) while Lazarus is taken to 'Abraham's bosom.'

The parable of a Pharisee and a tax collector praying in the temple appears in Luke 18:9-14. The Pharisee, proud and superior, thanks God that he is not like the despised tax collector; the tax collector on the other hand, will not lift his eyes, but pleads for mercy as a sinner. The Lord is very pointed in His conclusion.

> "I tell you that this man, rather than the other, went home justified before God. For everyone who exalts himself will be humbled and he who humbles himself will be exalted." (Luke 18:14)

Again we see the role reversal. The humble will be raised up while the arrogant will be cast down.

We meet another tax collector in Luke 19:1-10 – a real one this time, Zacchaeus. Luke records that the people 'muttered' that the Lord was going to be the guest of a 'sinner,' but after Zacchaeus repents and offers to recompense those he has cheated, the Lord concludes:

> "Today salvation has come to this house, because this man, too, is a son of Abraham. For the Son of Man came to seek and to save what was lost." (Luke 19:9-10)

The idea of seeking and saving the lost is prominent in Luke. Before the parable of the lost son in Luke 15, we read about the lost sheep and the lost coin and the conclusion to both parables is essentially the same:

> "... there will be more rejoicing in heaven over one sinner who repents than over ninety-nine righteous persons who do not need to repent." (Luke 15:7)

To Luke, the message of the gospel is sent not only to the chosen elite, but also to those who were considered least in Jewish society, to Gentiles and to other marginalised individuals. Mark also, writing primarily for Gentiles, does not lay emphasis on the priority of Israel. It is Matthew, writing for Jews, demonstrating that the Lord Jesus is the fulfiller of Old Testament prophecy, sent to the lost sheep of the house of Israel, Son of David and Son of Abraham, who focuses his attention on the Lord's coming to Israel. However, even Matthew, with his Jewish emphasis, does not exclude Gentiles from the Lord's blessing. The first people to visit the young child, in Matthew's account are the Magi – astrologers, who came to pay homage to the king of the Jews. The Canaanite woman is blessed, when (or perhaps because) she recognises her position as a "dog." Although Matthew emphasises the priority of Israel, and the fact that the Lord's ministry was primarily for them, it is by no means an elitist message – Gentiles and other outsiders are also included in Israel's blessings. There is thus a unity among the first three gospels – they contain a similar message, albeit with different emphases.

However, the Gospel of John is very different in structure and aim.

The unique approach of the fourth Gospel

John's purpose in writing

As indicated earlier, John's purpose in writing the fourth gospel is explicitly stated in 20:30-31:

> Jesus did many other miraculous signs in the presence of his disciples, which are not recorded in this book. But these are written that you may believe that Jesus is the Christ, the Son of God, and that by believing you may have life in his name.

The "signs" in the gospel are therefore a major key to understanding John's message but there are four basic aspects of the Lord and His work that John uses to demonstrate that He is "the Christ, the Son of God." These are:

Eight signs

John structures his gospel around a number of miracles that Jesus performs – seven signs during His public ministry and one after His resurrection[7]. These signs demonstrate:

- His power over the processes of nature (turning water into wine; walking on the water, the miraculous catch of fish).
- His ability to spontaneously create (feeding the 5,000).

---

[7] For a detailed discussion of the signs in the Lord's public ministry, see *The Signs in John's Gospel* by W M Henry, published by The Open Bible Trust.

- His power over disease (three healings).
- Perhaps greatest of all, His power over death, when He raised Lazarus, as a foretaste of His own death and resurrection.

However, more importantly, they were a major part of the evidence that He was the Christ since Isaiah had prophesied that He would perform these signs:

> Say to those with fearful hearts, "Be strong, do not fear; your God will come, he will come with vengeance; with divine retribution he will come to save you." Then will the eyes of the blind be opened and the ears of the deaf unstopped. Then will the lame leap like a deer, and the mute tongue shout for joy. (Isaiah 35:4-6)

The Jewish leaders, who knew their Scriptures well, should have recognised Him.

Seven discourses

The gospel also contains seven major discourses in which Jesus debates with the Pharisees and sets out His message to the people. In these debates Jesus makes a number of stupendous claims for Himself. For example, he claims that:

- He is the Son of God (3:16-20).
- He is the giver of eternal life (3:15).
- He has been given authority to judge the human race and to raise the dead (5:21-23).
- He pre-dates Abraham (8:58).
- He has the power to lay down His life and take it up again (10:18).

In addition to the claims that He makes for Himself, Jesus introduces authoritative teaching in these discourses that is not gleaned from the Law and the Prophets. For example:

- He tells the woman at the well about the nature of true worship (4:21-24).
- He scandalises the Jews by revealing that the very things in which they trusted – the Scriptures and Moses – would condemn them because they spoke about Him (5:39-40,45-47).

The source of the Lord's teaching was His Father and John demonstrates this clearly by explaining the clash of authority in Jesus' dialogues with the Jews. In these debates the Lord makes astonishing claims for Himself and supplements them with revolutionary teaching that subverts the Pharisees' regulations-based codes. This was no ordinary man. The Jews tried to discredit Him – He was Joseph's son (6:42) and they ridiculed Him as demon-possessed and raving mad (10:20). But many who met Him put their faith in Him.

His private teaching

In chapters 14-17 we have a section in which the Lord teaches His disciples privately. Following the demise of Judas, He gathers the remaining disciples and gives them intimate, personal information about the relationship between Himself, His Father and the Holy Spirit and, even more strikingly, how the disciples can be made part of that relationship. The section closes with the Lord praying to His Father for Himself, for His disciples and for those who will subsequently believe through their message. His prayer is for unity among believers, so that they may remain in that secure relationship with Him and His Father.

This is the most fascinating part of the gospel and it is written by an eyewitness, who was there at the time. The depth of the teaching in this section is tremendous and by including it here, John really brings out the fact that Jesus is the Christ, the Son of God.

Individuals' reaction to meeting Jesus

Throughout the gospel, John introduces his readers to a number of people who encounter the Lord Jesus and who realise that He is, in fact the Christ, the Son of God. Their testimony is recorded for the benefit of those who have never met Him in the flesh. These include:

- John's own testimony as an eye-witness in the first and last chapters of the gospel.
- The testimony of John the Baptist in 1:32-34.
- The reactions of Andrew, Philip and Nathanael to meeting Jesus (1:40-51).
- Nicodemus, who met Jesus in chapter 3 and subsequently helped Joseph of Arimathea to bury His body.
- The woman at the well, whose understanding of Jesus' identity progressed from an ironic "Are you greater than our father Jacob?" (4:12) to "Could this be the Christ?" (4:29).
- The man born blind who acknowledged Jesus as Son of Man and worshipped Him (9:38). No first century Jew would worship anyone other than God, and no Jew would accept such worship, so there is no doubt as to what is being claimed here by the Lord Jesus.

In this way John provides personal endorsement of the events he is describing and introduces us to people who have encountered the Lord and who were convinced of who He is. He has set the evidence before us. How will we respond? Christ told Thomas:

> "Because you have seen me, you have believed; blessed are those who have not seen and yet have believed." (John 20:29)

And that includes us. We will be blessed with forgiveness and eternal life if we believe.

Conclusion

Conclusion

If God has seen fit to inspire four different accounts of the time the Lord Jesus spent on earth, it should not surprise us that there would be considerable differences between them. However, when we stand back and look at the picture each one has painted, we can see that they do have a significant amount in common.

The gospels all describe Him coming to Israel as their Messiah, proclaiming to them the nearness of the kingdom of God. John the Baptist came before Him to prepare the way, as Isaiah had foretold. Christ's teaching and the miracles He performed were His credentials as Messiah; the people, and especially the religious leaders, should have recognised Him as such.

Why did they fail to do so? Partly it was due to the fact that Jesus was not the type of Messiah they were anticipating; they were looking for a military leader who would liberate them from the Romans and restore the kingdom to the nation. Instead, they found someone who was gentle and humble in heart (Matthew 11:29) and who was prepared to lay down His life for His sheep (John 10:15).

They thought they knew Him – He was just the son of Joseph the carpenter, just an ordinary man from Galilee, without education. Their inability to recognise Him was also a result of their entrenched, institutionalised religion which they were not willing to disturb. The Lord Jesus condemned the religious leaders as hypocrites, vipers and the children of Satan himself. But in rejecting Him, the Jews were only following in the footsteps of their forefathers, who persecuted the prophets whom God had earlier sent to them. The Lord Jesus pronounced God's judgment on Jerusalem in Matthew 23, not in a tone of anger but of anguish:

> "O Jerusalem, Jerusalem, you who kill the prophets and stone those sent to you, how often I have longed to gather your children together, as a hen gathers her chicks under her wings, but you were not willing. Look, your house is left to you desolate." (Matthew 23:37-38)

Yet, although His coming did not result in the establishment of the kingdom of God, His mission was not a failure. As it became apparent that the nation was not going to believe in Him, the Lord began to concentrate on those who did. The latter parts of all the gospels record His teaching of the disciples and other believers, to prepare them for the coming events. Although they would be devastated by His arrest, trial and execution, their sorrows were to be turned to joy by the glories of His resurrection and ascension, followed by Pentecost and beyond. Life on earth was never going to be the same again.

It is wonderful to think about the mysteries that the four gospels reveal to us – that the Creator of the universe became a man to reveal the Father to us. Anyone who has seen Him has seen the Father, as He reminded Philip (John 14:9). He came to show us what God is like. Not only so, but He came to die, so that the way back to God could be opened up to those who believe.

The Lord came as the Christ - Israel's Messiah. He was the King of the Jews; He was the Son of Man and Son of God – which means He was Emmanuel, God with us.

John brings these ideas together as he sums up the purpose of his gospel.

> Jesus did many other miraculous signs in the presence of his disciples, which are not recorded in this book. But these are written that you may believe that Jesus is the Christ, the Son of God and that by believing you may have life in his name. (John 20:30-31).

May we believe and may that life be ours.

Appendix: The Dating of the Gospels

Appendix: The Dating of the Gospels

It is not uncommon to read that the Gospel of John was written in about AD 90 or that Mark wrote his gospel in AD 68. However, such dates are questionable.

If we consider first the three Synoptic Gospels. It is generally considered that the order of writing was Mark first, then Matthew and finally Luke. We also know that Luke wrote the Acts of the Apostles. That concludes with Paul being in Rome under house arrest, which is dated about AD 61-62. Acts 28:30 records he spent two years under house arrest, and says no more about Paul. So Acts was published about that time; approximately AD 63-64.

However, Luke wrote and published his gospel *before* he wrote the Acts of the Apostles. We may not know how much earlier, but definitely some time earlier and it would probably be safe to say that Luke's Gospel was published before AD 60. As Matthew was written before Luke, and Mark before Matthew, we can safely say that both of these were written some time before AD 60. Thus all three synoptics were written during the period of time covered by the Acts of the Apostles. But what about John?

We have seen that John wrote his gospel to convince his readers that "Jesus is the Christ, the Son of God" and he bases his argument and evidence upon 'miraculous signs' (John 20:30-31). Now such miracles as those prophesied by the Old Testament, e.g. those we have mentioned from Isaiah 35:4-6, could only be 'signs' to those who knew those Scriptures. Thus the miracles could not have been 'signs' to the Gentiles of that time as they did not know the Jewish Scriptures.

Not only that, we see that often miracles confused Gentiles. For example, when Paul healed a crippled man in Lystra the people of that city looked upon him and Barnabas as the pagan gods Hermes and Zeus and wanted to make sacrifices to them (Acts 14:8-13). Similarly on the island of Malta, where the Gentiles thought Paul to be a god (Acts 28:3-6).

However, John's desire to make Jesus known as 'the Christ, the Son of God' was exactly what was being preached to the Jews during the Acts period. For example, Peter proclaimed it to the Jews on the Day of Pentecost (Acts 2:31-32) and the Apostles taught it in the temple courts and the houses in Jerusalem (Acts 2:42). In the synagogue in Damascus Paul proved that Jesus was the Son of God, the Christ.

> At once he [Paul] began to preach in the *synagogues* that *Jesus is the Son of God.* All those who heard him were astonished and asked, "Isn't he the man who raised havoc in Jerusalem among those who call on this name? And hasn't he come here to take them as prisoners to the chief priests?" Yet Saul grew more and more powerful and *baffled the Jews* living in Damascus by proving that *Jesus is the Christ.* (Acts 9:20-22).

Similarly in the synagogue in Thessalonica (Acts 17:3). Also, we read that in Corinth, "Paul devoted himself exclusively to preaching, *testifying to the Jews*, that Jesus was the Christ" (Acts 18:5). Apollos did the same, "He vigorously *refuted the Jews* in public debate, proving from the Scriptures that Jesus was the Christ" (Acts18:28).

We see, then, that this was an issue for the Jews of the 1st Century; not for the Gentiles of that era. It would seem that John's Gospel was written to Jews and for Jews.

Not only that, we have a specific statement in Scripture that John was to minister to the Jews.

> James, Peter and John, those reputed to be pillars, gave me and Barnabas the right hand of fellowship when they recognised the grace given to me. They agreed that we should go to the Gentiles, and they to the Jews. (Galatians 2:9)

Both James and Peter address their letters to the dispersion, the Jews scattered throughout the Roman Empire and beyond (James 1:1; 1 Peter 1:1) and John wrote to a similar audience.

His gospel may have been written especially to support the work of people like Paul and Apollos whose ministry took them to the Jews of the dispersion, those who lived outside the land of Israel and were scattered amongst the nations.

If this is the case not only was John's Gospel written before the destruction of the temple in Jerusalem (about AD 70), but also before the prophetic judgement upon Israel recorded in Acts 28:25-27. There Israel, because of their hardened heart towards Jesus, rendered themselves blind to the significance of the miracles and deaf to the arguments from Scripture, and so God's Salvation was sent to the Gentiles (Acts 28:28).

Thus it seems highly likely that all Four Gospels were written fairly close together, during the period of time covered by the Acts of the Apostles.[8]

---

[8] For more detail on the dating of John's writings see Appendix 2 of Michael Penny's *Approaching the Bible* and *John: His life and writings,* both published by the Open Bible Trust.

More on the Gospels

The Message of the Synoptics

By W M Henry

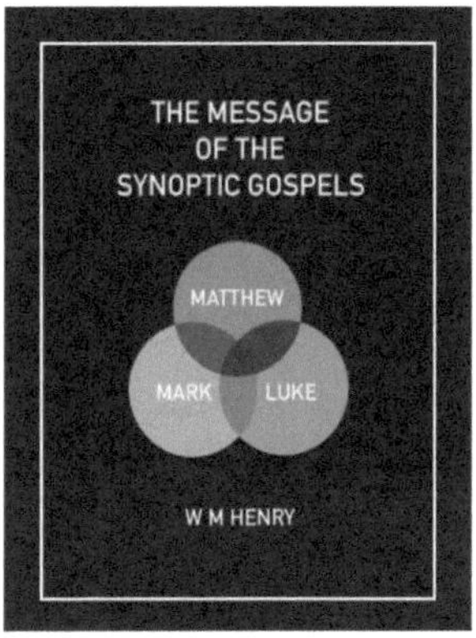

This book examines the earthly ministry of the Lord Jesus, as set out in the first three Gospels — the so-called 'Synoptic' Gospels — in its dispensational setting. The Lord, preceded by John the Baptist, came to Israel as foretold by Isaiah and other prophets, as the nation's Messiah, and to take His place on the throne of His father David.

He came preaching that the people should repent because the Kingdom was at hand. But what was the nature of that Kingdom and what were the criteria for entry to it? And what are the implications of Jesus' death, resurrection and ascension for the establishment of the Kingdom?

The book explores the Synoptic Gospels through seven chronological phases, each marking a different stage in the Lord's earthly ministry, and will provide Christian readers with a clearer understanding of the nature of His mission to Israel and beyond.

About the authors

William Henry was born in Glasgow in 1949. He qualified as a Chartered Accountant and worked in the accountancy profession before entering academia, where he spent 25 years in teaching and research. At present he is an education consultant working with undergraduate and postgraduate students. He lives in Glasgow with his wife and two daughters. He is an international speaker and has spoken in Canada, Australia and the Netherlands.

Michael Penny was born in Ebbw Vale, Gwent, Wales in 1943. He read Mathematics at the University of Reading, before teaching for twelve years and becoming the Director of Mathematics and Business Studies at Queen Mary's College Basingstoke in Hampshire, England. In 1978 he entered Christian publishing, and in 1984 became the administrator of The Open Bible Trust.

He held this position for seven years, before moving to the USA and becoming pastor of Grace Church in New Berlin, Wisconsin. He returned to Britain in 1999, and is at present the Administrator and Editor of The Open Bible Trust. In 2010 he was elected Chairman of Churches Together in Reading, where he speaks in a number of churches of different denominations. He is also a member of the Advisory Committee to Reading University

Christian Union and a chaplain at Reading College. He lives near Reading with his wife and has appeared on Premier Radio and BBC Radio Berkshire many times. He has made several speaking tours of America, Canada, Australia, New Zealand and the Netherlands, as well as others to South Africa and the Philippines. Some of his writings have been translated into German and Russian.

Both authors have written a number of publications.
Details of these can be seen at

www.obt.org.uk

For a full list of books available from
The Open Bible Trust,
please visit

www.obt.org.uk

Michael Penny is editor of *Search* magazine
and W M Henry is a regular contributor

For a free sample of
The Open Bible Trust's magazine *Search,*
please email

admin@obt.org.uk

or visit

www.obt.org.uk

Also by W M Henry and Michael Penny

Who is Jesus?

The Will of God: Past and Present
In the Bible and in the 21st Century

Sit! Walk! Stand!
The Christian life in Ephesians

Following Philippians
A Verse by verse exploration and discussion

For further details of these four, and other books, please visit

www.obt.org.uk/books

They are also available as eBooks from Amazon and Apple
and as KDP paperback from Amazon

Further Reading: Galatians

Galatians: Interpretation and Application
Michael Penny

This is a verse by verse historical commentary with modern day applications. The author's comments fall into two categories: historical and practical.

- First, he brings Galatians to life by considering the historical interpretation of each passage.
- Then, once that has been established, he has applied the teaching of that passage to Christians today.

It is important that we understand first what these writings meant to the people to whom they were initially written, before we seek to apply them to ourselves. If we do not do this, then we are in danger of misapplying the Scriptures.

Also available as an eBook from Amazon and Apple
and as KDP paperback from Amazon

About this book

The Four Gospels

Compared and Contrasted

The opening section looks at the four different writers of the Gospels and discusses the reasons why they wrote and their aim in so doing.

Then follows two lengthy sections.

- The first compares the Gospels, looking at common subjects and themes.
- The second, however, contrasts them, looking at the differences and suggesting reasons why the authors either decided to leave out certain events and discourses, or why they wanted to include them.

These two sections are well illustrated with ten tables showing clearly the similarities and the differences.

The book concludes with a helpful appendix on dating the Gospels.

Publications of The Open Bible Trust must be in accordance with its evangelical, fundamental and dispensational basis. However, beyond this minimum, writers are free to express whatever beliefs they may have as their own understanding, provided that the aim in so doing is to further the object of The Open Bible Trust. A copy of the doctrinal basis is available at

www.obt.org.uk/doctrinal-basis

or from:

THE OPEN BIBLE TRUST
Fordland Mount, Upper Basildon,
Reading, RG8 8LU, GB

Made in United States
Troutdale, OR
05/07/2025

31164182R00056